P9-APX-495

WOULD YOU
SURVIVE?

H. Becker

Scholastic Canada Ltd.
Toronto New York London Auckland Sydney
Mexico City New Delhi Hong Kong Buenos Aires

Scholastic Canada Ltd.
604 King Street West, Toronto, Ontario M5V 1E1, Canada

Scholastic Inc.
557 Broadway, New York, NY 10012, USA

Scholastic Australia Pty Limited
PO Box 579, Gosford, NSW 2250, Australia

Scholastic New Zealand Limited
Private Bag 94407, Botany, Manukau 2163, New Zealand

Scholastic Children's Books
Euston House, 24 Eversholt Street, London NW1 1DB, UK

www.scholastic.ca

Library and Archives Canada Cataloguing in Publication
Becker, Helaine, 1961-, author
Would you survive? / H. Becker.
ISBN 978-1-4431-4601-2 (pbk.)
1. Survival--Juvenile humor. I. Title.
PN6231.S886B43 2015   jC817'.6   C2015-901893-5

Cover illustrations copyright © Shutterstock, Inc.: background (Ursa Major), left (Anton Brand),
centre (Anastasiia Sorokina), right (murphy81).
Interior illustrations © by Shutterstock.com; pages 52–53 by Simon Kwan
copyright © Scholastic Canada Ltd.

6 5 4 3 2 1   Printed in Canada 121   15 16 17 18 19

MIX
Paper from
responsible sources
FSC® C004071

Table of Contents

Introduction 5

What's Your Survival Strategy? 6

Can You Find Your Way in the Wilderness?. 10

Pick Your Poison — or Not! 13

Polar Peril. 17

First Aid 101. 20

Would You Survive in a Fantasy World? 23

Are You an Ancient Greek Hero? 26

Would You Survive in a Scary Movie?. 30

Attack of the Intergalactic Microbes!. 33

Robin Hood or Scaredy Cat? 36

Fear Factor 40

Lord of the Flies Challenge 43

The Espionage Exam 46

Would You Survive a Computer Meltdown? 49

Escape to Planet Gewurtz 52

Desert Disaster 54

Will You Survive Middle School? 57

Reign of Terror 60

Cat-astrophe! 62

Can You Survive Stardom? 64

Game Show Elimination Round 67

Game Show Final Throwdown 69

Kidnapped by Pirates 71

Are You Fit Enough to Survive?. 74

Would You Survive Wizarding School? 78

Natural Disaster Survival Kit. 81

You're the Gladiator 84

Mini You. 87

Mother Goose Meets Her Match 90

Will You Survive Summer Camp? 93

Introduction

Would you survive an attack by intergalactic microbes? Attack of the robot overlords? What about sentient robots? Ghost cats? Sharknado? See how you stack up against evil masterminds, giant scorpions and the neighbourhood bully. You'll rate your bravery, your confidence and your muscle power. You'll also find out if you can master your own inner demons. Readers tip: Don't turn the page without a firm grip on your stuffed animal's paw. You'll need every extra bit of bravery-boosting possible.

What's Your Survival Strategy?

There's more than one way to be a survivor.
Find out which survival strategy best suits your
personality and temperament.

1. The power plant's nuclear core is melting down!
   You . . .
   a. jump up on a desk and shout, "You — call
      security. You — shut down sector 6. You —
      bring me a sandwich, STAT."
   b. figure out the fastest way to the exit.
   c. grab your buddy and together, tackle the
      loudmouth who's shouting on the desk, so
      everyone else can concentrate.

2. Your canoe has tipped! You . . .
   a. scan the water ahead for rocks and other dangers.
   b. single-handedly right the canoe.
   c. scan the water for your fellow canoers. Make sure everyone is
      safe before you try to salvage the canoe.

3. Towering inferno! You . . .
   a. gather everyone on your floor around you, then lead them down
      the staircase to safety.
   b. agree to check every
      room on the floor for
      stragglers, then meet up
      with your friends, who
      have already alerted the
      firefighters to the blaze
      and scouted out the
      safest location to wait for your rescuers.

   c. determine the best plan to get everyone out alive, and your odds
      of succeeding.

4. Your entire family has been swallowed by a whale! You . . .
   a. get everybody to exhale in unison, thereby forcing the whale to burp you to freedom.
   b. tell stories to keep everyone calm.
   c. figure out that if you wait a few weeks, the whale will be in Hawaii. And if you tickle its tummy at just the right moment, it will barf you up on the beautiful beach at Kona.

5. There is only one slice of pizza left. There are three of you, and you are all close to starvation. You . . .
   a. figure out, based on each person's size and weight, what percentage of the pizza they should be given.
   b. divide the slice into three equal pieces.
   c. decide who is strongest and who is weakest. Then divide the pizza between the two strongest (one of them being you, of course).

6. It's the final game of the playoffs. Victory is in your grasp! So is defeat. You . . .
   a. grit your teeth, take control of the game and score the winning goal.
   b. encourage everyone to do their best, then get out there and play your hardest.
   c. determine who is the most reliable player in a clutch and make sure he gets the most chances to score.

7. Plague! You . . .
   a. figure out a plan for distributing vaccines and vital food and medical supplies to the worst-affected areas.
   b. pull together a team of volunteers to keep the water supply clean and quarantined patients isolated.
   c. join the medical team to care for patients.

8. A grizzly has entered your campsite! You . . .
   a. gather everyone together in one tent. There's safety in numbers.
   b. get a good look at the grizzly and determine it's really after something to eat. So you hurl your backpack full of hamburger meat and buns toward the bear.
   c. get between the other campers and the bear, puff yourself up to your largest and scream as loud as you can.

9. You've been assigned a team project at school on Mayan hieroglyphs. You . . .
   a. take control of the project and tell everyone else what to do.
   b. figure out which parts of the project — the outline? the poster? — will count for the most marks and encourage the team to focus on those.
   c. do whatever tasks no one else likes to do.

10. You and your friends have been sent on a quest to find the sacred Snippet of Screed. You . . .
    a. research everything about the Snippet.
    b. gather supplies for the quest and make sure all the gear is in snip-worthy condition.
    c. appear on TV as often as you can to drum up support — and funds — for your quest.

SCORING

1. a3 b1 c2	4. a3 b2 c1	7. a1 b3 c2	9. a3 b1 c2
2. a1 b3 c2	5. a1 b2 c3	8. a2 b1 c3	10. a1 b2 c3
3. a3 b2 c1	6. a3 b2 c1		

HOW YOU RATE . . .

10-17 Strategist. You are the one who uses your huge honkin' brain to determine what needs to be done and figure out how to do it. You don't waste energy angling for the spotlight or making nicey-nice with everyone else. You focus on the essentials. As a result, you are likely to spot dangers before others do and avoid pitfalls that swallow up your less thoughtful, less analytical co-survivors.

18-24 Team player. You know that cooperation and collaboration are the most reliable avenues to success. You are great at obtaining and sharing information, and you also know how to build alliances — which is the kind of team-building skill that will save your bacon time and time again. You know that the sum of the parts is greater than the whole and recognize that the whole group's success may in fact depend on your ability to bring people together. Luckily, your charm and warmth ensure your survival!

25-30 Leader. You have confidence and charisma. As a result, people look up to you and listen to you. So when you take the lead, they follow! This can be both a good thing and a bad thing. What if you are heading in the wrong direction? Luckily, with your uncommon common sense, you know how to assign key roles to the right people. You then trust your lieutenants to do their jobs well, knowing you will all come out on top!

Can You Find Your Way in the Wilderness?

You've been out hiking in the wilderness with some friends. Suddenly you realize you're alone! Where did everybody go? You have no idea which way camp is, either. You are — *GULP* — lost. You do, however, possess some basic knowledge about how to figure out where you are — don't you? Answer true or false to each question to find out if you will survive!

1. If the moon rises after midnight, the more brightly lit side will be facing east.
2. In the morning, if you face the sun, north will be on your left.
3. The North Star is part of the Big Dipper constellation.
4. In the southern hemisphere, you can use the star called Polaris as a guide at night, since it always points south.
5. Moss always grows most vigorously on the north side of a tree.
6. In the northern hemisphere, the sun is due north at noon.
7. You can use a watch with hands as a compass in a pinch.
8. A bottle of water and a box of Smarties can be rigged up to make a compass.
9. When you are lost, you're always safer if you keep moving, in any direction, than if you stay put.
10. You've figured out the direction you need to head. To keep the correct bearing as you walk, you pick a landmark some distance away that lies on that bearing. When you get there, you check your bearing again, choose a second landmark and repeat.
11. To call for help, use the common distress signal: three shouts or short blasts on a whistle.
12. If you come across water, follow it! Your chances of meeting up with another person are greater near water than away from it.

SCORING

Give yourself one point for each correct answer.

1. True.
2. True.
3. False. It's part of the Little Dipper. The scoop of the Big Dipper points toward the North Star.
4. False. Polaris is the North Star and is only visible in the northern hemisphere. In the southern hemisphere, the Southern Cross can be used as a guide.
5. False.
6. False.
7. True. In the northern hemisphere, lay the watch flat on the ground and point the hour hand at the sun. Draw an imaginary line halfway between the hour hand and the 12. The line will point south. In the southern hemisphere, point the 12 toward the sun and find the line between it and the hour hand. Don't forget to adjust your watch to account for daylight savings time!

8. False.
9. False.
10. True.
11. True.
12. True.

HOW YOU RATE . . .

0-4 Bo Peep's sheep. Your way-finding skills need some work. Never leave home without a certified guide!

5-8 Signs point to . . . danger. Brush up on your way-finding skills before setting out in the wilderness.

9-12 Navigation expert! You always know exactly where you are.

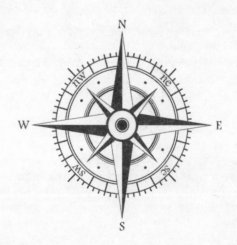

Pick Your Poison — or Not!

You're in the wilderness. You're hungry. But your food rations were washed away in the flood! You eye your surroundings for something, anything, edible. If you chow down on those chokecherries, will you survive? Take this quiz to find out.

1. The plant in front of you looks like wild carrot — very edible. Then again, it could be wild parsnip — also very edible. Or — *EEP!* — it could be poison hemlock. What do you do?

    a. Take a taste. If it doesn't burn your lips or taste bad, keep eating.

    b. Boil it up in a stew. That will get rid of any poison if you guessed wrong.

    c. Give it a pass.

2. The first step in the Universal Edibility Test is . . .

    a. a contact test. You crush the plant part against the skin on the inside of your wrist and wait for fifteen minutes to see if there is any negative reaction, like a burning or itching sensation.

    b. a taste test. You chew a tiny piece of leaf and see if it tastes bitter or foul.

    c. a burn test. You set the leaf on fire and see if it makes a bright flame.

3. Avoid eating any plant that . . .

    a. smells like almonds.

    b. smells like walnuts.

    c. smells like cotton candy.

4. Which group includes three plants that are safe to eat?
   a. Pokeweed, purslane, sassafras.
   b. Wild strawberry, water lily, horse chestnut.
   c. Burdock, cattail, chestnut.
5. True or false: You can boil the sap from several trees to make a sweet liquid that you can drink.
   a. True. Consider maple trees, birch trees and sycamore trees as likely options.
   b. True. But only maple trees will work.
   c. False.
6. You're stranded on the beach! Can you eat the seaweed?
   a. Yes. But avoid the stuff washed up onshore.
   b. No. It contains toxic chemicals that will make you grow a beard overnight.
   c. Yes. But don't eat too much on an empty stomach or you'll get a nasty case of the runs.
7. Plants with thorns are . . .
   a. generally safe to eat.
   b. painful.
   c. generally not safe to eat.
8. Steer clear of plants with . . .
   a. shiny leaves.
   b. flowers in groups that look like umbrellas.
   c. both a and b.
9. The berry from the yew plant is . . .
   a. one of the most dangerous berries of all. It might even kill you! Don't eat!
   b. a pretty nasty berry. It won't kill you, but it will make you very sick. Don't eat.
   c. a pretty berry.

10. The berries of the deadly nightshade plant are ...
    a. deadly.
    b. safe to eat. The leaves are what's deadly.
    c. non-existent. This plant does not have berries.

11. Chokecherries are ...
    a. deadly. If you eat them, you will choke to death within minutes.
    b. safe to eat. They're one of the most important food plants in traditional First Nations' diets.
    c. related to poison ivy.

12. You have just come across a bush covered with what look like delicious wild blueberries. Can you eat them?
    a. Yes. It looks like a wild blueberry so it's safe to eat.
    b. Maybe. But without knowing what it is for sure, you wouldn't want to risk it without doing a safety test.
    c. No. It looks like a blueberry, but is actually a deadly booberry.

13. The most dangerous wild plants are ...
    a. berries.
    b. mushrooms.
    c. wild grapes.

14. If you think you've eaten something poisonous, you should ...
    a. call 9-1-1 and tell them what was ingested.
    b. make yourself a sandwich.
    c. make yourself lie as still as possible until help comes.

SCORING

Give yourself one point for each correct answer.

1. c	4. c	7. c	10. a	13. b
2. a	5. a	8. c	11. b	14. a
3. a	6. c	9. a	12. b	

HOW YOU RATE . . .

0-3 Died on the vine. You've been poisoned! So sad.

4-7 Survived by a root hair. You've narrowly avoided consuming a foraged salad made of poison hemlock, ivy and oak.

8-12 Walkin' on the wild side. You have some basic knowledge of how to avoid eating poisonous plants. Now if only you knew as much about how not to get lost in the wilderness!

13-14 Food forage ace. You have a healthy respect for wild plants and possess the knowledge and common sense to avoid accidentally offing yourself by eating a gnarly mushroom or wicked weed.

Polar Peril

Your bush plane has had to make an emergency landing north of the tree line. Everyone else on the plane has been knocked unconscious, so you're on your own! Will you survive in the bitter, cold terrain of the tundra?

1. The wreck of the plane is smouldering. You fear it might explode! What do you do?
   a. Run as far away as possible!
   b. Move away from the plane, but make sure to keep close enough that you can return to it. Searchers will find you more easily if you stay near it.
   c. Cross your fingers. A nice big fire would help keep you toasty warm.
2. Which is your most valuable resource to help you stay alive?
   a. The plane itself. You can use it for shelter.
   b. Your wits. You can figure out how to radio for help.
   c. Your teddy bear.
3. You should wear a hat...
   a. whenever your head feels cold.
   b. all the time, even when sleeping.
   c. never. It traps cold air next to your head.
4. You're so thirsty! Can you eat some snow?
   a. Yes, as long as it's clean.
   b. Yes. It's water!
   c. No. You should melt it first so you don't get hypothermia.

DEHYDRATION

5. What's one good way to melt snow for drinking water?

   a. Put it in a leak-proof container (if you have a plastic bag, or zipper baggie, great!) and tuck it inside your coat so your body heat can melt it.

   b. Light a huge bonfire so the snow around it will melt.

   c. Put it in the microwave. Make sure to use a microwave-safe container!

6. You have a choice of gloves or mittens for your hands. You choose ...

   a. gloves. They give you more flexibility for doing all the chores you will need to stay alive.

   b. mittens. They keep your hands warmer.

   c. It doesn't matter. Gloves and mittens are both good protection.

7. You have frostbite if ...

   a. your skin is tingling and turning white.

   b. your skin is tingling and turning pink.

   c. your skin is cold and clammy.

8. You are thinking about trying to cross a small, frozen lake to reach an abandoned cabin for shelter. The ice may be safe to cross ...

   a. if it's blue.

   b. if it's grey.

   c. What are you thinking? You just survived a plane crash and now you're going to risk drowning?

9. How many calories will you need to consume every day to survive in the cold?

   a. 1,000 or fewer. You use less energy than normal in colder temperatures.

   b. 1,500 to 2,000 calories. About the same as you might use in warmer climates.

   c. 5,000 or more. It takes a lot of fuel to keep your body warm in frigid temperatures!

10. The greatest threat to your survival will be . . .

    a. hypothermia — being unable to maintain your core body temperature.

    b. polar bears — they are canny predators.

    c. frostbite.

SCORING

Give yourself one point for each correct answer.

1. b	3. b	5. a	7. a	9. c
2. a	4. c	6. b	8. c	10. a

HOW YOU RATE . . .

0-3 Cold, colder, coldest. You'd best stay home, by the fire, in your footie pyjamas.

4-7 Getting warmer. You have a 50/50 chance of surviving your polar peril.

8-10 Hot stuff! You've not only survived, but you've managed to save the bush pilot and the rest of the passengers too!

First Aid 101

Do you know what to do in an emergency?
Test your basic first aid IQ and find out.

1. Your friend has fallen off the slide! What's the FIRST thing you do?
   a. Check for danger. Is someone else coming down the slide? Get everyone, including your friend, out of the way.
   b. See if your friend can hear you by shouting loudly in her ear.
   c. Call for help.

2. Your little sister has tripped and her right knee is bleeding. You . . .
   a. get her to press down on the wound with her clean or covered hand to stop the bleeding.
   b. blow on the wound to clear any dirt out of it.
   c. cover the wound with a bandage and hope the bleeding stops.

3. You have a nosebleed! You . . .
   a. look up to the sky and pinch your nostrils until the bleeding stops.
   b. sit down, bend forward and pinch your nostrils until the bleeding stops.
   c. blow your nose to get the blood out.

4. You stayed out in the sun too long and now you have a sunburn. You . . .
   a. cover it up so it doesn't get worse.
   b. apply vinegar to make it feel better.
   c. soothe it with a cool, wet cloth or by running cool water on it.

5. The first rule in any emergency is to . . .
   a. call for help.
   b. keep calm.
   c. take control of the situation.

6. How would you treat a contusion?
   a. Bandage it.
   b. Ice it.
   c. Suture it.
7. If you think someone is choking, but he is breathing or coughing, what should you do?
   a. Nothing. Watch and wait — the object may come out on its own.
   b. Slap the person on the back.
   c. Do the Heimlich manoeuvre.
8. Your friend has banged her head! How do you know if she has a concussion and needs medical treatment?

   a. If she blacked out or was knocked unconscious, it's a concussion.
   b. If she seems confused or dizzy, it's a concussion.
   c. You can't always tell right away if a person has a concussion. She needs to be observed for at least twenty-four hours. In the meantime, she should rest.
9. Your friend has just been stung by a bee! How do you know if he is allergic and needs medical attention?
   a. He has hives or a rash that spreads beyond the site of the sting.
   b. He has trouble breathing.
   c. Either a or b.
10. Which group contains three items that should be in a first aid kit?
   a. Calamine lotion, alcohol wipes, chocolate bar.
   b. Non-latex gloves, hand sanitizer, blanket.
   c. Bottled water, instant cold compress, blood pressure gauge.

SCORING

Give yourself one point for each correct answer.

1. a	3. b	5. b	7. a	9. c
2. a	4. c	6. b	8. c	10. b

HOW YOU RATE . . .

0-3 Second aid superstar. You tend to respond like a chicken without a head in an emergency. Calm down, take a deep breath and bone up on basic first aid techniques.

4-6 Johnny on the spot. You have a good grip on basic first aid. Just be careful not to turn your patient into a mummy with your enthusiastic bandaging technique.

7-10 First responder. You keep a cool head in an emergency and know how to take care of simple, common first aid tasks. You get a very gentle fist bump!

Would You Survive in a Fantasy World?

1. You are taking your pet unicorn for a walk when a band of merry men leap out at you. What do you say?

    a. "Robin, my good buddy! Great to see you again! How fares my sister, the lovely Maid Marian?"

    b. "Uh-oh," and try to hide your million-dollar ride behind you, since Robin is a notorious thief.

    c. "Nice tights, dude."

2. The Evil Lord of Sauronia has just blasted the Shore with a veil of Dark that smells like black licorice. What do you do?

    a. Gather your furry-footed friends around you and make a plan to bake cookies.

    b. Gather your furry-footed friends around you and make a plan to make a run for the opposite coast.

    c. Gather your well-armed (and furry-footed) friends around you and make a plan to defeat the Evil Lord using cherry-scented arrows.

3. The Knights of the Round Table are having an argument. They have asked you to judge who's right! What do you do?

    a. Side with King Arthur. 'Cause he's, like, the king.

    b. Side with the hero, Sir Lancelot.

    c. Side with Merlin since he's the one with all the magic powers and can turn you into a tree frog.

4. You went to sleep in your own bed. But while you were dreaming, fairies came and stole you away to their kingdom under the hill. What do you do?

    a. Find the Fairy Queen and show her your cool arm fart skills.

    b. Look for the secret door back to your own world. It's gotta be here somewhere . . .

    c. Use your incredible human cleverness to try and trick the Fairy Queen into letting you return to your own realm.

5. You have come into possession of a magic cauldron. What do you do with it?

   a. Make a big honkin' pot of chili. The big football game is tomorrow!

   b. Brew up some vile magic potion that will turn your enemies into kangaroos with bunions.

   c. Go on a quest to find the true owner.

6. A wizard has gifted you with an invisibility cloak! What do you use it for?

   a. Robbing a bank.

   b. Sneaking onto the ice at an Oilers game and scoring the winning goal!

   c. Saving Rapunzel.

7. You must choose sides in the battle between Orcs and Porcs. Which do you throw your lot in with?

   a. The Orcs, because they have some seriously awesome fangs.

   b. The Porcs, because they have some seriously awesome bacon.

   c. The Dorks, because no one even realizes they are part of the battle. Bet they have all the totally cool tech and will win it all.

8. You have been sent on a quest for the Golden Hyena. What do you do?

   a. Laugh.

   b. Get your rubber boots — it's gonna be messy.

   c. Prepare your enchanted arrows and polish the shield you were given by High King Weaselus. You will come back victorious or not at all!

9. You walk through a wardrobe and find yourself in a snowy wasteland dominated by a lamppost. What do you say?

   a. "I must be in Narnia, again! Can't wait to see my old pal, Tumnus!"

   b. "Whoa, I must have eaten too much of that smelly brie at dinner. It's given me cheese nightmares." Then go back to sleep.

   c. "I'm gonna miss *Antiques Roadshow* now!" Then look for the way back to the wardrobe.

10. The Dwarf King has decided you shall be First Knight of the Under-Realm. What will be your weapon of choice?
   a. A war-hammer forged of Dwarvish iron.
   b. A crossbow forged of Dwarvish gold.
   c. A very cranky skunk.

SCORING

1. a10 b5 c1
2. a3 b8 c6
3. a4 b2 c12
4. a5 b3 c0
5. a8 b5 c10
6. a2 b5 c6
7. a4 b1 c8
8. a3 b5 c6
9. a8 b3 c10
10. a5 b7 c9

HOW YOU RATE . . .

25-50 Newt. Your instincts for survival are slim to none. Luckily you are a slippery fellow, and eye of newt has gone out of favour as a magical ingredient. Cultivate patience. If you can stay out of sight long enough, you will grow into a fearsome dragon and will be able to exact revenge on all those evil elves who called you "Fig Newton" on the elvish playground.

51-70 Sorcerer. Or is that Sauce-erer? You have what it takes to survive the tough challenges of Fantasyland or to be a chef in a 2-star restaurant. Increase your chances of making it home in one piece by boning up on your deboning technique. Keep your knives sharp, your apron clean and your crockpot set to "Liquefy Enemies."

71+ Dragonslayer. You not only survive the perils of Fantasyland, you ARE one. You kill knights, dwarves and dragons alike with your really long, really boring stories. Merlin, Sauron, Voldemort and the White Witch have joined forces to try and craft a magic muzzle that will shut you up once and for all!

Are You an Ancient Greek Hero?

Those crazy Olympians, messing around with people like they were mere mortals. Oh, wait. Being that you are a mere mortal, do you have what it takes to be a hero, raised to the status of demigod? Or will you be ground under Zeus's heel and served to Artemis's dogs for their dinner, like everyone else?

1. Your mother has made you impervious to harm by . . .
   a. making you take a bath once a week, whether you need it or not. > Go to question 2.
   b. crafting you armour out of the souls of hermits. > Go to question 3.
   c. teaching you how to run like crazy at the first sign of danger. > Go to question 4.
2. The Goddess of Love is sitting on the end of your bed! She confesses she has a tremendous crush on you. She offers you immortality in exchange for one kiss. You . . .
   a. toss Herman, your stuffed alligator, at her and she dissolves in a puff of twinkly smoke. > Go to question 6.
   b. close your eyes and pucker up. Wow — immortality! > Go to question 10.
   c. refuse. Because, gross. > Go to question 11.
3. You find yourself in a giant labyrinth. Or maybe it's actually a barn — *hoo-ee* — does it smell! You . . .
   a. check your pockets for string so you can find your way out. > Go to question 8.
   b. check your pockets for hay. Your buddy, the minotaur, is always grateful for a snack. > Go to question 9.
   c. check if you have a signal on your phone. You do! Use your GPS to find your way out. > Go to question 10.

4. You wake up to discover a giant tinfoil caribou sparkling on your front lawn. You . . .

   a. drag it into the house to take a closer look at it. > Go to question 5.

   b. add antlers and twinkling lights — instant holiday decorations! (So what if it's July?) > Go to question 6.

   c. have a good laugh, then open the door in the caribou's behind to invite your crazy prankster pals in for pancakes. > Go to question 7.

5. Which would you prefer to have?

   a. The ability to turn people to stone with one look, like Medusa. > You are PERSEUS.

   b. Wings, like Icarus. > Go to question 11.

   c. Really, really bad fish breath, like Poseidon. > Go to question 12.

6. The God of War is mad at you. You . . .

   a. tell him to act his age and get over it. > You are HECTOR.

   b. say, "Sorry, sir, that I knocked down your Lego tower. It was an accident and won't happen again." > You are TED THE PLUMBER.

   c. call your best pals, the God of Goof and the God of Doof, as backup. > Go to question 10.

7. How would you describe yourself?

   a. As strong as an ox. > You are HERCULES.

   b. As clever as Einstein. > You are ODYSSEUS.

   c. As charming as the Lucky Charms leprechaun. > You are ACHILLES.

8. Would you like to be king?

   a. Of course! > You are THESEUS.

   b. Nah, too much work. > You are TED THE PLUMBER.

9. Which would you prefer?
    a. Engaging in a battle of wits. > You are ODYSSEUS.
    b. Engaging in a battle of strength. > You are HERCULES.
    c. Taking a nap. > You are TED THE PLUMBER.
10. True or false: EVERYBODY knows your name.
    a. True. > You are HERCULES.
    b. False. > You are THESEUS.
11. You have a huge amount of homework to do. You . . .
    a. procrastinate. > You are THESEUS.
    b. dig right in. > You are HERCULES.
12. You prefer . . .
    a. competition. > You are ODYSSEUS.
    b. collaboration. > You are HECTOR.

MEET THE HEROES . . .

Achilles. You have a weird obsession with feet. You are ridiculously brave, ridiculously strong and ridiculously good looking. Only problem is you are also ridiculously unlucky. So even though you possess heroic qualities, you really have to look both ways when crossing the street and beware of things like arrows, minotaurs and mouldy cheese. Avoid: golden apples, cities beginning with the letter T.

Hector. You always root for the underdog, don't you? Perfectly understandable since, as Troy's great warrior, you lost the most famous battle *ever*. Don't feel bad, though; in your current life, you are seriously due for success. Expect to conquer the entire world! Avoid: wooden horses, people named Achilles, Greek salad.

Hercules. So you have some pretty impressive attributes for an ordinary kid. You are brave enough to cannonball off the high dive and clever enough to beat your five-year-old cousin at Candyland. Watch your step, though — if the Olympians start watching you, you'll be cleaning out their disgusting stables for the next millennium. Avoid: arm-wrestling matches, mountaintops in Greece.

Odysseus. You are the wiliest hero of them all — so clever you can defeat sorceresses, one-eyed monsters and foot-long sub sandwiches without raising a sweat. You have a terrible sense of direction, though, so make sure to always carry a compass with you — even to the washroom. Avoid: ships, sirens.

Perseus What? They never told you? News flash: your father wasn't *really* a shower of gold. You're actually part Olympian — but which part is still a mystery. It might be your cracked sense of humour (courtesy of that funster, Hades), or your freakishly giant earlobes. All we can say is your life is sure to be — *ahem* — interesting. Avoid: snake-headed monsters, mirrors, getting a swelled head.

Ted the Plumber. Alas, the Olympians do not consider you worthy of notice. The good news is they probably won't mess up your life. Not much, anyway. Avoid: battles with beasts bearing more than one head, long journeys to the underworld, annoying anyone with wings.

Theseus. So you defeated the minotaur and founded the city of Athens. Big deal. What are you going to do for your next hero trick? With your flair for the dramatic, it will probably be something amazing! Like going down to the underworld to rescue a beautiful maiden, or sailing off with the Argonauts. Then again, you might just get straight As and an NHL contract. Avoid: mazes, caves, bungee jumping off high cliffs.

Would You Survive in a Scary Movie?

The house: haunted. The stairs: creaky. Will you make it out of this scary movie alive?

1. You are caught in a freak thunderstorm. A ramshackle house, alone on a hill, looms. You . . .

   a. grab the giant knocker on the front door and bang.

   b. knock, instead, on the door of the sweet little cottage made out of — yes! Candy!

   c. huddle under a tree, praying you will not be struck by light— *ZZZZZZT!* Ow!

2. You are alone in your house. You hear a mysterious noise from upstairs. You . . .

   a. call 9-1-1.

   b. squeeze your teddy bear's paw.

   c. go up the stairs calling, "Hello? Anyone there?"

3. You are in a hotel that is mysteriously empty of guests. An over-the-hill movie star with a demonic laugh offers to check you in. You . . .

   a. ask for your room key.

   b. back away, slowly, so you don't attract the attention of the man-eating spiders amassing at your feet.

   c. get a really, really bad feeling that you are trapped in a scary movie.

4. Which is scarier?

   a. Paddling a canoe across a dark, haunted lagoon in the dead of night. Alone.

   b. A doll that looks like a clown.

   c. A castle with a laboratory in the attic.

5. You are with a group of friends at a cottage when the lights go out. You...

   a. go off by yourself to find the circuit breaker so you can turn the lights back on.

   b. scream until your face turns purple.

   c. do nothing. Power failures happen all the time up at the lake.

6. A mysterious cloaked man who took refuge in your house during a blizzard left your dad a key in a strange box, saying, "Keep this safe until I return and you will be rewarded. But if you mess with it, you will be seriously sorry." Your friends dare you to retrieve the key from the box. You...

   a. get the key and use it to pick your teeth. That guy was a nutter.

   b. get the box, show them the key, but don't touch it. That guy looked like he hadn't washed his hands since 1665.

   c. Seriously? You're not going anywhere near that key! It's cursed!

7. Your sister's head starts to spin and a strange, deep voice comes out of her mouth. You...

   a. say, "Nice one!" and give her a fist bump.

   b. sigh and reset her head. This happens all the time, especially if she gets hungry.

   c. freak out, of course.

8. You come across a mysterious green mask. You put it on and it takes over your body and soul! You are...

   a. grateful — you now have the best Halloween costume ever!

   b. determined — to rid yourself of this evil at any cost!

   c. disappointed — you wish your evil, soul-destroying mask were red, or black, not a silly Kermit-ish green.

9. You suspect evil lurks in the basement of Hill House. You and two friends grab flashlights and head down the stairs... in what order?

   a. You go first — because the monsters always come from behind.

   b. You go last — because you'd like your pals to get eaten before you do!

   c. You go in the middle — because you are the monster!

10. A vampire and a zombie are having it out at the coffee shop. You . . .
    a. hang around to see who wins.
    b. try to calm them both down — we're all civilized monsters here!
    c. call your pal Frankenstein to sort them out.

SCORING

1. a5 b10 c3	4. a5 b10 c2	7. a5 b10 c2	9. a0 b5 c0
2. a10 b5 c1	5. a5 b2 c1	8. a3 b5 c7	10. a3 b1 c5
3. a5 b8 c2	6. a3 b5 c10		

HOW YOU RATE . . .

18-30 Bait. You attract ghosts, evil demons and other monsters with sickening regularity. But you haven't yet figured out how to escape from them or destroy them. Write your will.

31-50 Demon food. You have a few survival skills, but they mostly involve screaming like a ninny and freezing in panic. Luckily you seem to emit frequent bursts of cabbage scent. (Did you have Brussels sprouts for dinner?) So the monster-movie villains tend to stalk right past you and chomp down on your friends.

51-70 Demon stalker. You have a solid sense of when to lay low and when to call those monsters' bluff. You know how to keep calm in a crisis and have a solid sense of strategy. (Don't open that door!) You may actually get out of Hill House/Dracula's Castle/Tomb of Doom alive.

71-80 Demon demolisher. Are you sure you didn't write the script for this scary movie? You laugh in the face of danger, mostly because you can see it coming from a mile away. Why open the closet? There's obviously a murderous puppet waiting inside. And only a fool would follow a hunchbacked guy named Igor into the shadowy gloom. Monsters quake when they see you coming because they know you can turn them to dust with the snap of your fingers and the crack of your wit.

Attack of the Intergalactic Microbes!

Aliens are attacking! No, they don't have green skin or three heads. They are microscopically tiny infectious organisms — and out to get YOU!

1. You feel a burning sensation on the back of your neck. You . . .
   a. scratch it.
   b. immediately reach for your intergalactic microbe decontamination kit. Better safe than sorry.
   c. look at the back of your neck in the mirror.
2. Your space probe has returned from the surface of Glorp. You open the sample capsule and . . .
   a. get a face full of *eeeepridigdxx*. Game over.
   b. use the rare minerals you find in there to construct a biological weapon to destroy interplanetary life forms. *Mwa, ha, ha!*
   c. discover it is full of Glorp gunk and it smells like you-know-what.
3. The intergalactic microbes attack by making you think you have turned into a dog. You are immune because . . .
   a. you are already a dog — a fine specimen of a boxer, too, thank you very much.
   b. you've always been a cat person.
   c. you are an intergalactic microbe.
4. What is the best defence against intergalactic microbes?
   a. Washing your hands.
   b. Washing your feet.
   c. Washing intergalactic microbes.
5. An intergalactic microbe has entered your bloodstream. You can only get rid of it by . . .
   a. singing "Mary Had a Little Lamb." In Russian.
   b. drinking ginger tea with a slice of lemon.
   c. riding the Red Rocket Roller Coaster 100 times in a row.

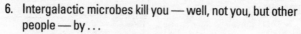

6. Intergalactic microbes kill you — well, not you, but other people — by . . .
   a. disrupting their brain function.
   b. disrupting their ability to tell a good joke.
   c. disrupting the class.

7. Intergalactic microbes multiply . . .
   a. at the speed of sound.
   b. at the speed of light.
   c. but have difficulty with division and fractions.

8. You've been sent on a last-ditch mission to save Earth from an invasion from you-know-whats. There's just you and your best friend, Rover, on the spaceship. You are approaching the microbial home planet when Rover says, "Woof!" You know that means . . .
   a. "I need to go walkies. Now."
   b. "I've got my stun gun set to 'Roll over, microbe!'"
   c. "You can do it, O Great One!"

9. Which is a symptom of intergalactic microbe colonization?
   a. The sky turns purple at sunset.
   b. It gets really, really dark out after supper.
   c. You develop an irresistible craving for bacon.

10. Intergalactic microbes are . . .
   a. 100 percent real.
   b. 100 percent made up by the author.
   c. your closest relatives.

SCORING

1. a1 b2 c3	4. a4 b3 c2	7. a2 b3 c5	9. a2 b1 c3
2. a1 b3 c2	5. a1 b3 c4	8. a1 b2 c3	10. a4 b1 c5
3. a5 b3 c1	6. a2 b4 c3		

HOW YOU RATE ...

13-21 Microbe mulch. You'll be first to go when the invasion happens. Don't worry — it will be painless (yeah, right).

22-30 Microbe middleman. You cannot be trusted — in the event of an intergalactic microbe invasion, you may just side with the microbes and betray your earthling pals.

31-39 Microbe master. Your quick reflexes, superhuman intelligence and incredible bravery will save Earth from invasion. In the meantime, you are in charge of world peace. Make it so.

Robin Hood or Scaredy Cat?

Most people are scared of *something*. And some fears are incredibly common — almost everyone has them. How do you compare? Are you braver than most, or a teeth-chattering, shivering bundle of nerves?

1. How many items on this list give you shivers?
   - Flying
   - Speaking in front of a group
   - Heights
   - The dark
   - Spiders

2. How many items on this list give you the heebie-jeebies?
   - Snakes
   - Enclosed places
   - Thunder and lightning
   - Dogs
   - Germs

3. How many items on this list make your heart beat fast and your palms sweaty?
   - Rejection
   - Failure
   - Being judged
   - Crowds
   - Being lost

4. How many items on this list could give you nightmares?
   - Clowns
   - Zombies
   - Monsters
   - Black cats
   - Sharks
5. Now think about the degree of your fears. Do any of the items you checked off . . .
   a. make it impossible to go on with your day if they are present or if you think about them too much?
   b. make you so uncomfortable you will go greatly out of your way to avoid them?
   c. make you uncomfortable enough that you will go a little bit out of your way to avoid them?
   d. None of the above.
6. Now think about how you cope with your fears. Choose as many answers as apply.
   a. Tell yourself your fears are unrealistic and don't let yourself get carried away.
   b. Practise self-soothing techniques, like taking deep breaths, when you feel frightened or nervous.
   c. Share your fears with others as a way to make them seem less threatening.
   d. None of the above.
7. Which of these statements best applies to you?
   a. You can control your fears.
   b. Your fears control you.

SCORING

1. Give yourself 1 point for each item.
2. Give yourself 2 points for each item.
3. Give yourself 3 points for each item.
4. Give yourself 2 points for each item.
5. a10 b5 c1 d-5
6. Take away 3 points if you chose a, b or c. Give yourself 5 points if you chose d.
7. Take away 5 points for a. Give yourself 5 points for b.

HOW YOU RATE . . .

-19-0 Seriously brave. Nothing scares you. Either you lie like a rug or you are uncommonly fearless. While this can be a useful trait, it can also get you into real danger. There are occasions when having some nerves is not only desirable, it can save your life. You *should* be afraid when you are standing at the edge of a steep cliff or when you hear the rattle of a snake under your boot!

1-30 Brave when you need to be. You seem to possess a sensible mixture of courage and caution. Sure, some things give you the creeps (zombies!) or make your heart flutter uncomfortably (sharks!). But you don't let your fears get in your way. You take a deep breath, laugh a little and change the subject. Tougher is overcoming your all-too-common social anxieties: fear of rejection, of speaking in public, of failure.

Remember: The more you challenge yourself in these areas, the easier it gets. And you're not alone! Fear of public speaking is one of the most common fears in the world.

31-60 Nervous Nelly. You see the world as fraught with peril — much of it heading right for you! As a result, you tend to avoid situations that make you uncomfortable. You'll turn off the TV to avoid seeing a scary movie, or decide not to run for student council because you can't stand the thought of being judged. This attitude does keep you safe, but it also limits you. The good news, however, is that your fears *can* be controlled. Sharing them with someone who cares about you is a good place to start. Before long you'll be the bravest kid on the block!

Fear Factor

An evil scientist is testing your nerve with a horrifying set of challenges. Each time you must make a choice between two terrifying tasks. Will your choices lead you out of the mad lab or straight to the morgue?

1. Which will you eat?
   a. A plate of live bees. > Go to question 2.
   b. A plate of dirty chicken feet. > Go to question 3.
2. Which will you choose? To swim through a pool that's infested with . . .
   a. piranhas. > Go to question 5.
   b. tiger sharks. > Go to question 4.
3. You must choose between . . .
   a. hot bamboo shoots under your fingernails. > Go to question 6.
   b. a series of twelve electric shocks, each one worse than the last. > Go to question 7.

4. Which will you choose?
   a. Staring down one ravenous lion. > Go to question 8.
   b. Outwitting 25 ravenous rats (while stinky cheese is strapped to your body). > Go to question 9.
5. Choose between being blindfolded while . . .
   a. walking a tightrope over a canyon. > Go to question 10.
   b. shooting the world's most dangerous rapids. > Go to question 11.
6. You prefer the evil scientist send in . . .
   a. the clowns. > Go to question 12.
   b. the dentists. > Go to question 13.

7. You must choose between wading through . . .
    a. a pit of vipers. > Go to question 14.
    b. a pit of black widow spiders. > Go to question 15.

8. The evil scientist places a hairy tarantula on your wrist and hooks you up to the scream-o-meter. How loud do you scream?
    a. Loud enough to make the spider jump. > Go to question 15.
    b. You don't scream. You whimper. > Go to question 14.

9. You must choose between . . .
    a. making a speech on medieval castle life to the evil scientist's 300 henchmen. > You make it out of the lab alive!
    b. bungee jumping from an airplane. > So sorry, the scientist pushed you one scream too far. MORGUE.

10. You prefer he test your nerve by . . .
    a. introducing flu germs into your cell. > Go to question 8.
    b. leaving you all by yourself for two days. > Go to question 9.

11. You must choose between . . .
    a. hyenas. > Go to question 12.
    b. crows. Lots and lots of crows. > Go to question 13.

12. He sets you free! You can try and run to the nearby boat and safety! Alas, along the way you will have to dodge . . .
    a. two crackerjack snipers. > Go to question 14.
    b. five zombies. > Go to question 15.

13. And now you must outrun . . .
    a. flowing lava. > So sorry. You're toast.
    b. a tsunami. > So sorry. You're drowned toast.
14. For your final challenge, you must choose to have . . .
    a. a scorpion placed on your face. > You survive! A little twitchier, to be sure, but you have made it out of the challenge lab alive!
    b. a leech placed in your armpit. > You survive! There's only one drawback — your nightmarish experience has turned YOU into a mad scientist!
15. You escape! You're being interviewed on TV! You die of stage fright. So sorry.

Lord of the Flies Challenge

You and a group of twelve classmates are shipwrecked. You manage to make it to a deserted island. Will you survive?

1. The first thing you do when you reach shore is . . .
   a. collapse on the beach.
   b. construct a shelter.
   c. ask if anyone's got a cellphone signal.
2. You are very thirsty, so you . . .
   a. drink some sea water.
   b. drink some water from the lagoon nearby.
   c. drink some rainwater that has collected in the base of a large flower.
3. The other kids start organizing themselves into groups. You will probably wind up with . . .
   a. the jocks.
   b. the brains.
   c. the outsiders who don't fit in with either the jocks or the brains.
4. Big Jo makes a plan for gathering firewood and making a signal fire. You think it won't work. You . . .
   a. say nothing.
   b. ridicule the plan.
   c. quietly suggest a better plan.
5. Big Jo starts making fun of one of the smaller, more timid kids. You . . .
   a. join in.
   b. say nothing.
   c. defend the little kid.
6. The shelter you build is . . .
   a. covered and off the ground.
   b. far away from the other kids' shelters.
   c. close to the beach.

43

7. You wear glasses. What do you use them for?
   a. Looking out for a rescue ship.
   b. As a lens to focus sunlight and start a fire.
   c. Alas, you lost them during the shipwreck.

8. A power struggle is going on between Big Jo and Top Dawg for control of your band of survivors. What do you do?
   a. Support Big Jo. He's a scary dude who's a loudmouth and a bully, but effective at command.
   b. Support Top Dawg. He's smarter and kinder, but not as effective as Big Jo.
   c. Lay low and stay out of it as much as you can.
   d. Try to take control yourself.

9. Kids start getting sick. You . . .
   a. run away from the group. It could be contagious!
   b. take care of the other kids.
   c. determine that the cause of the illness is the water they've been drinking. Get everyone to stop drinking from that green lagoon pronto!

10. Your greatest danger on the island comes from . . .
    a. wild beasts.
    b. exposure.
    c. Big Jo.

SCORING

1. a1 b3 c2	4. a1 b3 c2	7. a2 b3 c1	9. a1 b2 c3
2. a1 b2 c3	5. a2 b1 c3	8. a2 b3 c1 d2	10. a1 b2 c3
3. a2 b3 c1	6. a3 b2 c1		

HOW YOU RATE . . .

10-16 Lord of the fleas. You realize quite quickly that your greatest threat is a group that can't get along. Unfortunately, you decide the best way to handle this situation is to avoid trouble. But trouble has a way of finding you, doesn't it?

17-25 Sultan of survival. You are very good at avoiding trouble. Not so good at nailing down victory, though. Like most people, you tend to take the middle ground. If luck turns your way, you will survive, and even thrive! But a run of bad rolls and you'll be up the island's creek without a paddle.

26-30 King of the hill. You've got what it takes to survive this nightmare: A solid understanding of group dynamics, basic common sense and a healthy dollop of courage. You're not afraid to stand up for what you believe in or confront others who you see are making serious mistakes. You know it's not always the most pleasant course, and it can be risky! But on the other hand, dying of severe sunburn on a deserted island while two other kids battle it out for supremacy isn't exactly a picnic either.

The Espionage Exam

So you think you have what it takes to
be a secret agent? Test yourself on this
entrance exam to I C U Spy Academy and
find out if you make the grade.

1. You've been given a special assignment by
   special agent James Bond himself! You . . .
   a. puff out your chest and say, "Count on
      me, Jim!"
   b. take the assignment, or pretend to
      anyway, then skedaddle. You prefer a
      nice quiet life, thank you very much, over
      a life of mystery and mayhem.
   c. take the assignment, then do your
      task without comment — and without
      breaking a sweat.
2. Your assignment is to spy on Queen
   Boolaboola! To do so, you . . .
   a. disguise yourself as one of her
      attendants and hang around her private
      quarters.
   b. bribe one of her attendants to install a video camera and audio
      recorder in her wedding ring.
   c. pretend you are an important journalist and arrange an in-depth
      feature on her so you can spend a week interviewing her and
      following her around with a camera crew.
3. You are supposed to meet your contact at a local comic book shop. You
   have never met her. How will you recognize her?
   a. By a pre-arranged signal: "Do you carry the Ozymandias comic
      books here?"
   b. You'll recognize her easy-peasy. She'll be the one who looks like a spy.
   c. You'll ask, "So, are you my contact?" to everyone in the store.

4. What is a spy's most important tool?

   a. Ruthlessness.

   b. Discretion.

   c. A hot dog–shaped eraser that explodes when tossed into your enemy's pop.

5. You are offered a job by a rival nation-state spying on your own government. What do you do?

   a. Refuse the job.

   b. Take the job. It sounds like fun.

   c. Take the job, but become a double agent reporting on the enemy nation-state's interests.

6. The best spies are ...

   a. suave.

   b. mousy.

   c. athletic.

7. Which "cover" would suit you best in your spy career?

   a. Hollywood star.

   b. Internet mogul.

   c. Aid worker in war-torn regions.

8. Can you decode this phrase: "XY 2 BOR ≠2b C3PO?"

   a. Yes. It says, "You are boring me, C-3PO."

   b. Yes. It says, "To be or not to be." From *Hamlet*. With some other Star Wars junk and DNA data thrown in as a screen.

   c. No. It's too boring to bother figuring it out.

9. You would describe yourself as ...

   a. good at everything you do.

   b. not one to brag.

   c. both a and b.

10. If you were to get a tattoo, what would it be?

    a. Invisible — with the secret message from HQ embedded in it.

    b. I ♥ the CIA.

    c. Hello Kitty.

SCORING

1. a1 b2 c3
2. a2 b3 c1
3. a3 b2 c1

4. a2 b3 c1
5. a1 b2 c3
6. a3 b1 c2

7. a1 b2 c3
8. a0 b3 c0

9. a2 b3 c5
10. a2 c1 c3

HOW YOU RATE . . .

10-16 Out-of-order operative. You probably didn't realize when you signed up for spy school that there'd be exams. Or that skills like math and foreign languages were on it! While you love the *idea* of being a spy, you're not really cut out for the ongoing drudgery of listening to Russians talk about how bad their weather is, or delivering so-called secret messages to the post box.

17-25 Cleaning agent. You get bored easily, which is a problem for a spy. The most successful agents are the ones who know how to lie low for long periods of time, keep their mouths shut and their noses clean. Luckily, you also possess some excellent qualities for espionage: You are seriously loyal, seriously nosy and seriously forgettable. Well done, Agent Ho-Hum.

26-32 Call me Intrepid. You've got the perfect cover for a spy. Your incredible good looks, charm, versatility and athletic prowess mean everyone has their eyes on you, all the time. So who would suspect you are actually carrying out covert activities right out in the open? Er, the enemy, that's who. Which is why they've now got you tied up in a cell in Svrsk-Krbd. Good luck talking yourself out of this one, Intrepid.

Would You Survive
a Computer Meltdown?

Many of us have become so dependent on our computers and other tech that we've lost, or never developed, some basic life skills. Take this quiz to find out how likely you are to survive a total computer meltdown.

1. Do you know what direction you are facing *right this second,* without checking any external aids?

    a. Yes.

    b. Not a clue.

2. Do you know your best friend's phone number?

    a. Yes.

    b. No.

3. Can you draw a map of your route from home to school?

    a. Yes.

    b. No.

4. If you didn't know how to spell a word, how would you find out?

    a. Ask someone.

    b. Go to a dictionary.

    c. It doesn't matter how you spell it.

5. You're bored. Check off as many of these pencil-and-paper games as you know how to play.

    a. Dots and squares.

    b. Battleship.

    c. Tic-tac-toe.

    d. Hangman.

6. Can you read cursive handwriting? Can you write it?
   a. Yes to both questions.
   b. Yes to one but not the other.
   c. No to both questions.
7. Can you tell time on a clock with hands?
   a. Yes, easily.
   b. Yes, with difficulty.
   c. Not really.
8. How many people's birthdays (not including your own) do you know off by heart?
   a. Five or less.
   b. Six to ten.
   c. More than ten.
9. You've been assigned to memorize a 20-verse poem for school. How difficult will you find this task?
   a. Very difficult.
   b. A little difficult.
   c. Not that difficult.
   d. Easy.
10. You have to research the life and career of Roberta Bondar for a school project. Can you think of at least three different ways to find out the information?
    a. Yes.
    b. No.

SCORING

1. a1 b0
2. a1 b0
3. a1 b0
4. a2 b3 c0

5. Give yourself 1 point for each game you can play.
6. a5 b3 c0

7. a3 b2 c0
8. a1 b3 c5
9. a1 b2 c3 d4
10. a3 b0

HOW YOU RATE . . .

2-10 Technogeek. You love technology so much you want to marry it! You may be spending too much time, however, tied to your computer, game console or phone! Unplug more often and connect with the real world. You will be happier and healthier in the here and now, and save yourself a meltdown of your own during a computer meltdown.

11-20 Techo take it or leave it. Sure, you like settling in and playing video games, and you're totally comfortable with using technology for gathering information, finding your way and keeping track of everyday stuff like when your next soccer match is. But you can manage fine without tech — as long as your dad keeps your schedules and your friends don't mind when you forget their birthdays or addresses! You will survive a computer meltdown with only a few rough "patches."

21-30 Tech-not. You know that technology has great value, but you don't see the point in downloading your life into a device. You like to stay active and use your brain and your hands to explore the world directly. As a result you have developed real skills — a better memory, more self-reliance and the ability to make your own fun anywhere, anytime. You will easily survive a global computer meltdown, and you might even wind up taking over the world!

Escape to Planet Gewurtz

Earth has suffered a global catastrophe — it has been taken over by billions of incredibly cute kittens. Their evil henchmen, the cat-ladies, now rule!

Goodbye Kitty!

Flush formation!
Lose a crew member.

Asteroid belt!

Lose an engine.

Ex-planet Pluto

To save humanity, you and a crew of six dog lovers (plus Jupiter, your faithful spotted companion) have embarked on a one-way trip to Planet Gewurtz, where you hope to establish a new, cat-free colony.

The trip is long and fraught with peril. Can you find your way to Planet Gewurtz? And will you survive the journey?

Litter box black hole!

Rings of Saturn!

Lose a crew member.

Sirius
the dog star.

Planet Gewurtz

Desert Disaster

Your camel has conked out. It's one hundred kilometres to the next oasis. Will you survive in the blistering heat of the Sahara?

1. Your hat blew off in the dust storm. You . . .
   a. don't mind — it was a really ugly one your Aunt Agnes gave you.
   b. fashion a new one out of an extra T-shirt.
   c. chase after it.

2. It is 11 am. You figure you can get to the oasis in about 4 hours, if you're lucky. You . . .
   a. get going ASAP — the sooner you start, the sooner you'll arrive.
   b. decide to stay put — your camel might recover, and it will only take you one hour by camel!
   c. look for a rocky outcropping that you can sit under, out of the sun, until later in the day.

3. You have one litre of water. You . . .
   a. sip it a little at a time, when you feel thirsty.
   b. drink it all down right away — it might evaporate otherwise.
   c. save it for when you feel really thirsty.

4. You're feeling hungry. Luckily, you have plenty of food! You . . .
   a. stuff yourself — you burn lots of calories trying to survive in the heat!
   b. eat a little — just enough to keep your energy up.
   c. don't eat — it will dehydrate you.

5. When you think about your desert predicament, you . . .

   a. panic and weep — because you don't want to get baked to death.

   b. thrill to the adventure of it all!

   c. keep calm — because you're one cool dude.

6. You have figured out which direction to go and start trudging off that way. As you go, you . . .

   a. draw arrows in the sand to indicate your direction of travel.

   b. build little rock inuksuit to announce, "Lost Canadian!"

   c. sing, "Hi ho, hi ho, it's off to the oasis we go!"

7. Mini-oasis! What do you do?

   a. Drink from that oh-so-loverly-looking pool of water.

   b. Eat a whole bunch of dates from the conveniently placed date-palm.

   c. Trudge past — you know it's a heat-induced mirage.

8. You are becoming dehydrated! You . . .

   a. move slowly so you don't break a sweat.

   b. breathe with your mouth open.

   c. cover your mouth with a bandana and sit quietly in the shade until it's cooler out.

9. It's getting dark out! You . . .

   a. build a fire to stay warm.

   b. plan on travelling as far as you can during the twilight period.

   c. wait until it is completely dark — and nice and cool — to continue your journey.

10. A herd of camels is coming your way! You . . .

    a. run the other way — wild camels are carnivorous.

    b. wave your arms in the air — your rescuers are on their way!

    c. follow the camels at a safe distance — they know where water is.

SCORING

1. a1 b5 c1	4. a3 b5 c1	7. a1 b5 c3	9. a3 b5 c1
2. a1 b3 c5	5. a1 b3 c5	8. a3 b1 c5	10. a1 b5 c3
3. a5 b3 c1	6. a5 b3 c1		

HOW YOU RATE . . .

10-20 Desert dud. You are uniquely qualified for building tree houses and winning snowball fights. If camel-trekking is in your future, write your will.

21-42 Desert dude. You might actually make it to the oasis in one piece! You know that you need to stay covered up to prevent both sunburn and sunstroke. You eat sparingly, but regularly, ration your drinking water and stay put, in the shade, during the hottest part of the day. Too bad about your pet camel, though.

43-50 Desert conqueror. You are The Hot One, the one everyone else wishes they could be. Alas, you often wind up alone, as you must leave weaker ones to die. As you regretfully set off in the direction of the setting sun, they gaze upon you with hollow eyes, wishing only for one more glimpse of your hotness. You weep dry tears and carry on. For solitude is your destiny.

Will You Survive Middle School?

Microbes. Monsters. Maniacs. Meh. Every kid knows the true, ultimate challenge is surviving — *gulp* — middle school.

1. First day of middle school! You ...
   a. get there early to grab a locker in the best spot.
   b. get there right on time and discover the only lockers that are left are the ones near the boys' washroom. P.U.
   c. need someone to explain to you what a locker is and why you need one.

2. Your lunch on the first day of school will be ...
   a. sushi.
   b. a very ordinary turkey sandwich and a box of apple juice.
   c. a very delicious but stinky wrap filled with Limburger cheese and fried onions.

3. Homeroom means ...
   a. the place where your bed is.
   b. the place where you start your day in middle school.
   c. the place where you go for detention in middle school.

4. In middle school, it is totally not cool to ...
   a. drool.
   b. bring a teddy bear to class.
   c. both a and b.

5. You can sign up to play an instrument! Which one do you choose?
   a. Cello.
   b. Trumpet.
   c. Kazoo.

6. Kids are trading cards in the playground! They are . . .
   a. more competitive than you.
   b. more outgoing than you.
   c. your best friends.

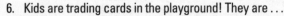

7. Your best friend, Catniss, wants to run for class president! You . . .
   a. try to drum up votes by wearing a bright red sweater and a cat-in-the-hat hat and running down the halls shouting, "THE CAT IS BACK!"

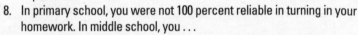

   b. decide to run too.
   c. make posters and help Catniss in every way possible.

8. In primary school, you were not 100 percent reliable in turning in your homework. In middle school, you . . .
   a. plan on acting the same way. It's worked for you so far!
   b. plan on doing your homework — if you remember.
   c. make a resolution to do your homework promptly every day and stick to it.

9. There's a kid in your class you don't like. You . . .
   a. avoid the kid.
   b. try to get changed to a different class.
   c. tell all your friends how much you can't stand that kid.

10. An older kid starts making fun of your name. You . . .
    a. ignore the kid.
    b. get really, really upset.
    c. own it. You might even get a hockey sweater made with the funny name on the back.

SCORING

1. a5 b3 c1
2. a3 b5 c1
3. a1 b5 c3

4. a1 b1 c5
5. a3 b5 c1
6. a5 b3 c1

7. a3 b1 c5
8. a1 b3 c5

9. a5 b3 c1
10. a3 b1 c5

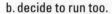

HOW YOU RATE . . .

10-20 Middle school maybe. Sure, it's a tough adjustment, but you can make it! Keep your sense of humour handy, and all will be well. Remember everyone else is struggling to find their place and fit in too.

21-42 Middle school maestro. You know middle school is just like primary school, just with taller kids. You take everything in stride. So what if you mess up now and then? Show me one kid who doesn't!

43-50 Middle school magician. You were BORN for middle school. You're the one who winds up running student council and starring in the school play. Did we mention captain of the hockey/soccer/softball teams?

Reign of Terror

You've been left to babysit your cousins — two-year-old triplets. Can you survive the toddler triple threat?

1. Huey knocked down Dewey's block tower! You ...
   a. put Huey in a time out.
   b. comfort Dewey.
   c. ask yourself, "Uh-oh. Where is Louie?"
2. Louie's face is scrunching up in a weird way. She ...
   a. is about to wail! You pick her up and comfort her.
   b. is about to make a you-know-what! You stand clear!
   c. is about to sneeze. You stand clear!
3. Bath time! How many rubber ducks can you juggle?
   a. 1.
   b. 3.
   c. 2 ducks, 4 tugboats and a toy T-rex.
4. Snack time! What's on your menu?
   a. Hot dogs, sliced into nice, soft, squishy circles.
   b. Cheese and gluten-free crackers.
   c. Nachos and spicy salsa.
5. How many times can you sing "The Wheels on the Bus" without your ears bleeding?
   a. Once.
   b. Ten times.
   c. Ooh! I love that song!

6. There is a giant snot bubble coming out of Dewey's nose. You ...
   a. wipe it away with a tissue.
   b. ignore it.
   c. screech, "Ew! Nose bubbles are revolting!"

7. Do you know all the words to "The Eensy Weensy Spider?"
   a. Yes.
   b. No.

8. Huey is pulling your hair. Dewey is swinging off your leg. Louie is shrieking, "Kitty! Kitty!" at the top of her lungs. You . . .
   a. are losing your mind. How much longer until backup arrives?
   b. are thinking about that cool video game you want to buy.
   c. are in heaven. Little kids are so much fun!

9. Playground time! Where is the best place for Huey, Louie and Dewey?
   a. The sandbox. You can keep an eye on all of them here!
   b. The swings. All three kids will be fastened into place on the baby swings.
   c. The slide. You can send them down one at a time.

10. Dewey won't stop crying! Which do you try?
    a. Singing and rocking her.
    b. Distracting her with a new toy.
    c. Both a and b. Plus silly faces, a snack and a horsey ride.

SCORING

1. a2 b3 c5	4. a1 b3 c2	7. a5 b1	9. a5 b3 c1
2. a1 b5 c2	5. a3 b1 c5	8. a2 b3 c5	10. a3 b2 c5
3. a1 b2 c3	6. a5 b1 c2		

HOW YOU RATE . . .

13-22 Toddler takedown. They got you good. You may never recover from your afternoon with the mini monsters.

23-32 Toddler tie. There were three of them and only one of you. Nevertheless you held your own. You live to see another day.

33-46 Toddler triumph. You have emerged victorious from your Trial of Terror. A little twitchy, perhaps, but victorious!

Cat-astrophe!

Well hello, kitty! You have nine lives! Can you make it to your first birthday — and full cathood — before all your lives expire?

1. Ooh! Ball of yarn! You . . .
   a. get tangled in it.
   b. bat it under the sofa.
   c. knit a cat hat with it.
2. Dog! You . . .
   a. bat it on the nose.
   b. curl up with it for a nap.
   c. run!
3. Goldfish in a bowl! You . . .
   a. stare at it fixedly for hours.
   b. overturn the bowl and eat that delicious fish.
   c. chase your own tail.
4. Can opener! You . . .
   a. run to the kitchen and do figure eights around the can opener's legs until she trips.
   b. go to sleep on the radiator.
   c. hiss at a flickering shadow on the wall.
5. Big, shiny car-shaped cat toy! You . . .
   a. chase it.
   b. ignore it.
   c. lick it.
6. Bedtime! You . . .
   a. curl up in an armchair.
   b. curl up in a shoebox.
   c. curl up on your owner's face.
7. Mouse hunt time. You . . .
   a. pounce!
   b. get distracted by a bird.
   c. get distracted by a human with hedge trimmers.

8. Robin on YOUR fence! You . . .

   a. watch it fixedly until it feels your evil and flees.

   b. pounce!

   c. ignore it.

9. Raccoon in the shed! You . . .

   a. lick paws.

   b. take it on. It's all about territory, people!

   c. yawn, find sunny spot for a nap.

SCORING

1. a0 b3 c5	4. a0 b3 c1	7. a5 b3 c0
2. a3 b5 c0	5. a0 b5 c3	8. a5 b0 c3
3. a5 b0 c3	6. a3 b3 c0	9. a1 b0 c5

HOW YOU RATE . . .

0 Curious cat. You have lost your life nine times. You did not survive to adult cathood. Don't worry — there is plenty of catnip in kitty heaven.

1-30 Fat 'n' happy. You not only survive to adult cathood, but you lead a very peaceful, very contented life as a human foot warmer.

31+ Top cat! You're king of the jungle — as long as the jungle consists of a human habitation, complete with litter box, Feline Feast treats and squeaky toys. Humans worship you. Other pets (that dopey dachshund — please!) bow-wow at your feet. Survival of the fittest — that's you.

Can You Survive Stardom?

Everyone says they want fame and fortune. But could you cut it as a big-time celebrity? Or would the paparazzi chew you up and spit you out faster than a three-day-old mackerel?

1. The real estate agent shows you a real estate. You know: 48-room mansion, 3 swimming pools, 500 hectares of prime oceanfront. You say . . .
   a. "Really? Is this shack all you have?"
   b. "Wowza! This place is perty!"
   c. "I'll take it for my weekend place . . . when I'm not in Monaco . . . or Bali."

2. You are nominated for an Oscar! You . . .
   a. sigh and complain, "Not again! It's *sooo* tedious to have to pretend to like people. I wish I could just stay home and watch TV."
   b. call your mother to tell her the good news.
   c. start writing your acceptance speech.

3. Someone posted a comment on social media saying they don't like your new hairstyle. You . . .
   a. call a press conference to complain about harassment by the media.
   b. record a new song about hair and donate the proceeds to your pet charity, Baldness Hurts.
   c. aren't on social media, so you don't even hear about it.

4. You've been asked to star in an action-adventure movie that is sure to be a box office smash! You . . .
   a. check your calendar. Too bad. It's filming the week you promised to play bingo with your grandma. Pass.
   b. check your calendar. You're free! You sign immediately and tell everyone you know how excited you are!
   c. demand the producers fit their schedule to yours because your workout regime is quite intense. And if they are very, very nice (they send you care packages of your fave candy, direct to your home gym!), you might agree to star.

5. Your rock band is getting back together again! You . . .
   a. announce you'll have nothing to do with it. You never liked those no-talents you used to call bandmates.
   b. commission a whole new stage wardrobe made of nothing but diamonds and LEDs.
   c. fret that you won't remember the words to the songs. It was so long ago.

6. You only eat . . .
   a. organic kale prepared by your personal chef to your precise instructions.
   b. champagne and foie gras, dahling.
   c. hamburgers. Nothing but hamburgers.

7. You are afraid of . . .
   a. flying.
   b. anonymity.
   c. Iowa.

8. Your favourite way to kick back and relax is . . .
   a. après-ski in Aspen, with 600 of your closest friends.
   b. at a party on a yacht with 750 of your closest friends.
   c. watching old *Zoboomafoo* episodes.

9. You meet your greatest rival at a restaurant! You . . .
   a. pretend you are the bestest friends in the world.
   b. stick out your foot to trip him as he walks by.
   c. storm out of the restaurant in a snit. You refuse to share your personal space with riff-raff.

10. You've spent all your fortune! You . . .
    a. quickly arrange a new comeback concert tour. You love your fans and they deserve this.
    b. marry someone younger and much, much richer than you. STAT.
    c. sue your manager, your record company and your personal psychic adviser.

SCORING

1. a3 b1 c5	4. a3 b1 c5	7. a1 b5 c3	9. a5 b1 c3
2. a1 b3 c5	5. a3 b5 c1	8. a5 b3 c1	10. a1 b3 c5
3. a3 b5 c1	6. a5 b3 c1		

HOW YOU RATE . . .

10-20 Swandive. You're really not cut out for celebrity. And who'd want it anyway? You'd much prefer a quiet life outside of the limelight, where people don't snap your picture at the supermarket and name their kids after you.

21-39 Flash in the pan. You have what it takes for stardom — of the very short-lived variety. Expect to be a one-hit wonder and invest your earnings in safe, dependable, boring stocks. What's wrong with Iowa anyway?

40+ Superstar! You redefine the meaning of the word. It now means, "THAT's obnoxious!" but who cares? You're the one with the flashy house, flashy car, flashy everything. And you're enjoying it all immensely, thank you very much.

Game Show Elimination Round

They're giving away a million billion trillion dollars on the game show *Greedy Guts*. All you have to do is survive the game show's Elimination Round against the other top competitors. Can you survive? Answer 12 out of the 15 questions on the Gut It Out Board. Then add up the points for each correct answer given to find out if you survive the elimination round and go on to the final Throwdown Round.

100-point questions
1. What is the capital of Norway?
2. $182 \div 13 = ?$
3. Water boils at ____°C.
4. The correct spelling of the word "riparian" is:
5. True or false: Amphibians don't lay eggs.

200-point questions
1. The Acropolis is in what city?
2. One-third of 300 is how much?
3. True or false: Plants make their own food.
4. Are bear and bare homophones?
5. Which is longer: a yard or a metre?

300-point questions
1. Ulan Bator is the capital of what country?
2. Which is greater: 67 x 7 or 58 x 9?
3. Your small intestine is part of what body system?
4. True or false: The word "disgusting" is an adjective.
5. On what continent might you find a sloth?

SCORING

100-point questions

1. Oslo
2. 14
3. 100
4. riparian
5. False

200-point questions

1. Athens
2. 100
3. True
4. Yes
5. A metre

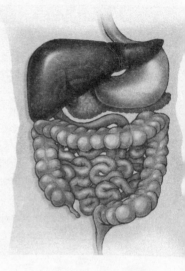

300-point questions

1. Mongolia
2. 58 x 9
3. Digestive system
4. True
5. South America

HOW YOU RATE . . .

0-900 Bye-bye. You really didn't want the money anyway, did you?

1000-1900 You've got enough guts! You squeaked through to the next round!

2000-2600 You've got plenty of guts! Move on to the next round, with a bonus starting score of 200!

2700 You've got the most guts of all! Move on to the next round, with a bonus starting score of 500!

Game Show Final Throwdown

You've made it to the Final Throwdown round on the game show *Greedy Guts*. You now have a chance to win a million billion trillion dollars — and keep it all for your greedy-guts self! There's no need to feel — *gulp!* — nervous! You've studied up and know the answer to everything, right?

Answer any five questions from the list below. Then turn the page to find out how many points each right answer is worth. See if your total is enough to survive and win the game.

1. $\frac{3}{6} + \frac{1}{2} = $ ___
2. True or false: Giant and enormous are antonyms.
3. The largest bird alive today is called the _____.
4. The capital of France is _____.
5. Canada has ___ provinces and ___ territories.
6. What sport is played with a "pigskin"?
7. Water freezes at ___°C.
8. How many baby teeth do humans normally have?
9. In the northern hemisphere, the longest day of the year falls in what month?
10. A "bonsai" is a kind of _____.

SCORING

1. 1.100 points
2. False. 200 points
3. Ostrich. 300 points
4. Paris. 100 points
5. Ten provinces, three territories. 200 points
6. Football. 200 points
7. 0°C. 100 points
8. 20. 300 points
9. June. 200 points
10. Plant. 300 points

HOW YOU RATE . . .

0-100 Sayonara. You were too busy running your multinational corporation to really pay much attention to this distraction, weren't you? It's okay, because you don't need the money anyway. You've already socked a million billion trillion dollars into your offshore bank account.

200-600 See ya later. Not bad. Not bad at all. Alas, your score wasn't quite good enough to win the big bucks. But never fear — you did well enough to be invited to play *Greedy Guts* again next year!

700-1200 Semi-success. You did it! You split the pot and win a billion dollars! Sorry it's such a pittance and you have to share. Better luck next time.

1300 HIGHEST SCORER EVER! You win the million billion trillion dollars! And you don't have to share it with anyone, not even your pet hamster.

Kidnapped by Pirates

Captain Black-and-Bluebeard has nabbed you and your buddies! Can you survive a buccaneer's brig?

1. One-Eyed Carl orders you to swab the deck. You . . .
   a. whack him in the head with the mop.
   b. jump overboard, using the mop as a flotation device, as you swim for shore.
   c. swab the deck.
2. Peg Leg Pete grabs your plate of piratey stew (don't ask what's in it) and starts eating it. You . . .
   a. tell him a story of someone you knew who died a miserable, painful death from a bad batch of the stuff.
   b. whack him with the mop you stole from One-Eyed Carl.
   c. steal a plate of stew from Sad Sack Sally, the kid who was kidnapped along with you.
3. The pirates are boarding another ship! You . . .
   a. cower in the brig, hoping for rescue.
   b. join the pirates in the attack. You've always wanted to swing from rigging and shout, *"Arrrr!"*
   c. quietly take command of the ship and sail away, leaving the pirates stranded on the other ship.
4. How do you feel about parrots?
   a. Love 'em.
   b. Love 'em cooked with tomatoes.
   c. They kind of give you the creeps. Those evil eyes, those sharp little beaks . . .

5. Black-and-Bluebeard wants to play a game of buccaneer baccarat with you. If he wins, he throws you overboard. If you win, he throws you overboard. You . . .
   a. make sure the game ends in a tie.
   b. regale him with such crazy stories he decides to keep you alive for another night, and another night, and another . . .
   c. cry like a baby, hoping he will take pity on you.
6. You sail through a storm. All the pirates are seasick! You . . .
   a. tend to them in their distress.
   b. throw every last one of 'em overboard. Look who's captain now!
   c. swab the deck, 'cause pirate puke is really gross.
7. Uh-oh! One of the ship's cannons is jammed. Captain Black-and-Bluebeard orders you to crawl inside it and clean it! You . . .
   a. agree, on the condition that you'll win your freedom if you are successful.
   b. refuse. You have no desire to become a human cannonball.
   c. secretly rig the cannon so it propels you safely across the water into a passing privateer's ship!
8. Which joke is funniest?
   a. What has eight legs and eight eyes? (Eight pirates!)
   b. Why are pirates so mean? (They just *arrrrrgh!*)
   c. How much does a pirate pay for earrings? (A buck an ear!)
9. You have managed to steal Black-and-Bluebeard's treasure map. You . . .
   a. wish you had paid attention in geography class! You have no idea where Brooklyn is! And what does that big red X over "the Bank of Brooklyn" mean anyway?

   b. commit it to memory and bide your time.

c. ask Black-and-Bluebeard if you can go halfsies with him.

10. You hear a ticking sound. You know that means . . .
     a. Captain Hook is somewhere nearby. Hide!
     b. a man-eating crocodile is somewhere nearby. Hide!
     c. you are still wearing the watch your great-aunt Zelda gave you
        for your birthday.

SCORING

1. a5 b0 c3	4. a3 b5 c1	7. a3 b1 c5	9. a1 b5 c0
2. a5 b4 c3	5. a2 b5 c1	8. a5 b4 c1	10. a5 b5 c1
3. a1 b3 c5	6. a5 b3 c2		

HOW YOU RATE . . .

12-20 Buried treasure. Black-and-Bluebeard buried your corpse with the loot so your ghost will guard it through eternity. Luckily you like the tropics, and there's a nice view.

21-39 Black and blue. You're bruised but alive. Well done, matey!

40-50 Captain Sweetie Pie! You not only survived the adventure, but have taken over the entire pirate fleet and the island of Jamaica. Practise your scowl though — it needs work.

Are You Fit Enough to Survive?

Life is challenging. Find out if you've got the physical skills to survive in a crisis.

1. You're in a prisoner-of-war camp. Can you dig your way out? To do so, you will need exceptional arm strength.
   Your challenge: Do as many push-ups as you can in one minute. (Don't forget to keep count!)

2. You've slipped into quicksand! Can you yank yourself from the pit of doom by grabbing onto an overhanging dead tree limb?
   Your challenge: Do as many chin-ups as you can in one minute. (Don't forget to keep count!)

3. You're on the 86th floor of a skyscraper when a fire breaks out on the 87th floor. There are 12 babies who need rescuing. Can you save yourself and the babies?
   Your challenge: Run up and down a flight of stairs 12 times without stopping.

4. You're being chased by a zombie horde! Will you outrun them?
   Your challenge: Run in place or do jumping jacks for two minutes without stopping.

5. Your cruise ship has sunk in shark-infested waters! Can you stay submerged, and out of sight, until the sharks leave the vicinity?
   Your challenge: Hold your breath for as long as you can. (Don't forget to keep track of your time.)

6. A killer clown is on the loose. You must hide and stay completely quiet until the most ridiculous danger ever has passed.
   Your challenge: Sit quietly without twitching, giggling, talking, coughing — you know, without doing *anything* — for three minutes. Try to keep your mind blank too.

7. You're skiing down Mt. Kookachoo when you hear the distinctive roar of an avalanche! Can you evade the snow, or will you become a snowball yourself?
   Your challenge: Do six forward rolls without stopping or rolling into anything.

8. You have to cross a very narrow but very, very deep chasm. It's about a metre across and 5,000 metres to the bottom. Oh, and there are ravenous wildebeests nipping at your heels. Can you make it across the chasm?
   Your challenge: Do a long jump. One really, really long jump. Have your tape measure ready!

SCORING

1. **Fewer than 4.** You better hope help arrives fast.
   4 +. You've dug your way to the perimeter and freedom!

2. **Fewer than 4.** Glub glub glub . . .
   4+. You've hauled yourself out — and your fourteen drowning pals too!

3. **Are you out of breath and panting like a beast after completing this challenge?** Too bad about those babies, eh?
   Are you pink-cheeked but feeling fine? You've saved yourself, the babies and forty firefighters too!

4. **Are you out of breath and panting like a beast after completing this challenge?** The zombies have eaten your brains.
   Are you pink-cheeked but feeling fine? You've outrun the zombies!

5. **30 seconds or less.** The sharks chow down on your tender flesh. Yum.
   31+ seconds. The sharks swim off and you are rescued!

6. **You *almost* got to three minutes**. So sorry, the clown will find you and kill you with really, really terrible knock-knock jokes.
   You lasted three whole minutes. So sorry, the clown will still find you and kill you with really, really terrible knock-knock jokes. You knew there's no escaping the psychotic clown, didn't you?

7. **You conked out before completing your six rolls, or you smacked into something**. You've been rolled over by a wall of powder.
   You completed six forward rolls safely. You did it! You're the sole roll survivor!

8. **Less than one metre**. Ooooops . . . *splat*.
   One metre or longer. It's not really nice to tease the wildebeests like that, now that you're safely on the other side of the chasm.

Would You Survive Wizarding School?

You have been selected by some mysterious wizardy process to enrol in the top wizarding school in your country, Wiz Academy Inc. Will you survive your gruelling first weeks as the new kid?

1. Do you have any scars?
   a. Yes — in the shape of the letter L on your forehead.
   b. Yes — a hot-dog shaped scar on your ankle.
   c. No.

2. Your favourite flavour of jelly bean is . . .
   a. lemon.
   b. cherry.
   c. earwax.
3. You've been given your new wand! You . . .
   a. immediately use it to turn your sister into a newt.
   b. immediately set the art room on fire. Oops.
   c. immediately start reading *How to Use a Wand — Level 1.*
4. Uh-oh. That popular kid is looking at you funny. You . . .
   a. use your wand to turn him into a newt.
   b. use your innate wizarding skills to bend him to your will and make him your minion.
   c. make a funny face back.
5. Which magic word is the most powerful?
   a. Mutatis!
   b. Please.
   c. Abracadabra!

6. You're about to be sorted into school teams for cribbage! You hope you wind up on which team?
   a. The Magic Cabbages.
   b. The Tiggywinkles.
   c. We Love Bacon.

7. Your first Potions class! What potion do you choose to make?
   a. Love Potion #9.
   b. Transmogrifying Milk.
   c. Fleap Formula.

8. Your best friend has accidentally caused you to sprout wings from your ears. You . . .
   a. turn *her* into a hairy apple. *Ha, ha, ha!*
   b. fly to France — because you can.
   c. say, *"Auris Alar Vo dee oh doh!"* and your wings disappear without a trace.

9. What is your secret protector beast that springs from your chest whenever danger threatens?
   a. A fire-breathing dragon.
   b. A winged cow.
   c. A turkey named Stuart.

10. Do you really want to be a wizard?
    a. You bet!
    b. Maybe — if you can always be home in time for supper.
    c. No way! You just want to be a regular kid.

SCORING

1. a5 b2 c1	4. a3 b4 c5	7. a1 b5 c3	9. a5 b3 c1
2. a3 b2 c5	5. a3 b5 c1	8. a1 b2 c3	10. a5 b3 c1
3. a3 b4 c5	6. a5 b3 c1		

HOW YOU RATE...

15-20 Wizard school dropout. Your wiz skills are abysmal. Luckily, wands are not required at beat box school. Where you will be the star student!

21-40 Wizard school worker bee. Your wizarding skills are iffy, but you keep your place at wizard school thanks to your incredible enthusiasm and extra-large trust fund — Headmaster Hedley truly appreciates that big donation your folks made to the school. Keep up the good work. You'll make an excellent sorcerer's apprentice someday.

40-48 Wizard school whiz. You not only survive wizarding school, you take it over and turn *everyone* — even Headmaster Hedley! — into your apprentices. As a result, you single-handedly bring about peace in our time and end hunger, thanks to your clever little dinner bell spell. Everyone wishes they were you, but sorry, they can't be.

Natural Disaster Survival Kit

Is yours packed?

1. You've received word of an impending sharknado! What do you do?
   a. Get out your snorkel and face mask.
   b. Get out your shark repellent.
   c. Tie yourself to the mast of a ship. It's gonna be a wild little ride!
2. You are caught in a thunderstorm. Lightning is striking the ground all around you! You . . .
   a. take your cheese sandwich out of your lunch box and place it under a tree. A well-timed lightning strike will toast it perfectly.
   b. get out your house key and a kite so you can reproduce Ben Franklin's famous experiment.
   c. use your phone's camera to record the storm. You're bound to get plenty of hits on YouTube!
3. A forest fire is roaring toward your town. Your house is smack in the fire's path! You . . .
   a. start cutting a fire break around the house.
   b. grab your plastic dinosaur collection and run for your life.
   c. don your fireproof safety suit. You bought it for moments just like this!
4. An ice storm has left you stranded on a country road, kilometres from shelter. You . . .
   a. build a snowman but kick it over when you realize you don't have a carrot for the nose.
   b. marvel at how pretty everything is!
   c. use your special sasquatch-summoning screech to call your BFF for help.
5. The volcano has erupted. Here comes the lava! You . . .
   a. get out your surfboard. You've coated it with fire-retardant chemicals so you can ride the lava wave!
   b. put on your jammies — they're fire retardant!
   c. keep your cool by eating as much ice cream as you can.

6. A magnitude 6.8 quake has just rocked your city. Buildings everywhere have collapsed. And the one you're in is creaking ominously! You . . .

    a. run out into the street, clucking like a chicken.

    b. stand under a door frame.

    c. head to the basement — you'll be safer there.

7. There are snakes on your plane — and they are venomous and angry. You . . .

    a. charm them with your hypnotic flute playing.

    b. grab a parachute and jump!

    c. tell the pilot to turn down the heat.

8. An indestructible robot monster has come to your town from the future and grabbed YOU by the scruff of the neck. You . . .

    a. ask it nicely to put you down.

    b. kick it in the shins.

    c. decide you are the only one who can save the world, and start bossing it around.

9. A tornado warning has been issued for your town. You . . .

    a. pack your bag. You always wanted to be transported to an imaginary realm of flying monkeys.

    b. pack your bag and bike over to the next town. If you're lucky, the tornado won't veer south.

    c. head to the basement. It's safer down there.

10. The black plague is swooping through your community! You . . .

    a. don't worry — you've been vaccinated.

    b. don't worry — you are immortal.

    c. don't worry — you've had the black plague already, and chicken pox was worse.

SCORING

1. a1 b2 c3
2. a3 b2 c1
3. a2 b3 c1
4. a2 b1 c3
5. a3 b1 c2
6. a2 b3 c1
7. a2 b1 c3
8. a2 b1 c3
9. a1 b2 c3
10. a3 b1 c2

HOW YOU RATE . . .

10-15 R.I.P.

16-24 Not dead yet . . . but nearly.

25-30 Sole survivor. So what if the planet is devastated. It's ALL YOURS!

You're the Gladiator

Don't ask how, but you've found yourself in the dank dungeons beneath the Roman Colosseum — in ancient Rome. Upstairs the crowds, including the emperor himself, are cheering for blood — your blood. Will you survive?

1. Your fellow gladiators are choosing straws for who will go first. You . . .
   a. knock the straws to the ground and volunteer to go first.
   b. slip away for an emergency trip to the washroom, er, back corner.
   c. close your eyes, cross your fingers and choose a straw.

2. Your first combat will be against two hungry bears. You . . .
   a. choose two super-sturdy spears and stuff a hatchet into your breastplate.
   b. run into the arena shouting, "Mom! Dad!" and scoop them up in a big bear hug. Because you are, in fact, a Russian black bear.
   c. choose two super-sturdy salmon and stuff a hive full of honey into your breastplate. You'll slay the bears after they've stuffed themselves on your tasty treats.

3. Your second combat will be against six vicious Nile crocodiles (a.k.a. "gladigators"). You . . .
   a. choose six sturdy spears and stuff a hatchet into your breastplate.
   b. shout, "Eeny, meeny, miny, moe. Catch a crocky by the toe!" as you enter the arena.
   c. look up where the Nile is on a map.

4. Next up: Chariot races! You . . .
   a. cheat.
   b. cheat.
   c. cheat.
5. Your third combat: Lion. You . . .
   a. choose twelve sturdy spears and stuff a hatchet into your breastplate.
   b. wish you had a supply of catnip!
   c. pay your good buddy, Dan, to take your place in the arena. He gets on really well with lions.
6. The empress has named you her favourite! That means you . . .
   a. get to attend a Roman feast before you are brutally slaughtered in the arena.
   b. get to retire from gladiatoring with your life intact!
   c. get on the wrong side of the emperor.
7. You've organized an uprising of the gladiators. You will free yourselves and escape! Your name is . . .
   a. Glad the Impaler.
   b. Spartacus.
   c. Inigo Montoya.

8. Fourth combat! You get to choose which type of game to play. You choose to . . .
   a. don a mask with no eyeholes and charge blindly at your opponent — on horseback.
   b. fight with two swords — but no armour. (Your opponent gets armour and one sword.)
   c. fight with a trident and a lasso. (You get armour, though!)
9. Fifth combat! You struggle against a giant named Isthisguyforrealius. He has you down on the ground! With his sword point at your throat! The emperor holds up a fist with his thumb tucked inside, out of sight. It means . . .
   a. you're spared!
   b. you're finished.
   c. the emperor wants a cheeseburger and fries.

10. Your final combat is against Hilarius, the emperor's own personal favourite. You . . .
    a. can't help but giggle. His name is, dare we say, hilarious.
    b. know he has won thirteen times straight! You gulp in terror. Mr. Giggles is a very good gladiator.
    c. know he won thirteen times straight! Laugh in glee. The odds are in your favour then, since most gladiators don't even make it to ten wins.

SCORING

1. a1 b5 c3	4. a3 b2 c5	7. a3 b5 c1	9. a5 b2 c1
2. a3 b1 c2	5. a3 b1 c5	8. a3 b4 c5	10. a1 b3 c5
3. a3 b5 c1	6. a5 b3 c4		

HOW YOU RATE . . .

5-20 *Sadiator*. You mercifully don't suffer much. Unless you consider having your throat removed by vicious beasts suffering.

21-39 *Madiator*. The emperor went to the "facilities" and missed your two incredible victories over Isthisguyforrealius and Hilarius. Which means you get to fight again! Good luck against Carpophorus, the infamous gladiator who killed twenty wild beasts single-handedly in one battle. And by the way, he doesn't like your face.

40-48 *Gladiator*. You have survived the gory world of gladiatorial combat! Now will you survive the notoriously bad Roman traffic to get home in one piece?

Mini You

You wake up one morning and discover something strange has happened to you in the middle of the night, because now you are tiny. Really, really tiny. Like, 15-cm-tall tiny. Will you survive?

1. Your first challenge: Get out of bed! You ...
   a. rip loose threads from your pillowcase to make a sturdy rope. Then toss it over the side of the bed and climb safely to the ground.
   b. climb down using the cleverly arranged Lego steps you placed beside your bed last night.
   c. jump. And pray.
2. Your dog Blooper thinks you are a new toy! He ...
   a. sniffs you.
   b. licks you.
   c. shakes you in his teeth.
3. You brush your teeth using ...
   a. a toothpick with a frayed end.
   b. a tiny plastic hairbrush you stole from your sister's dollhouse.
   c. some carpet fluff, which unfortunately tastes a little bit like cat.
4. What do you eat for breakfast?
   a. Three crumbs of toast and a medicine dropper full of milk.
   b. One piece of dog kibble and the water in the dish under a houseplant.
   c. One slice of banana, and it gives you terrible gas.
5. How do you get to school?
   a. Your best friend carries you in his backpack.
   b. You time it just so, make a running start and leap onto the bottom step of the school bus.
   c. You don't bother going to school. They don't teach "surviving cat attacks and other perils of being tiny" there.

6. Speaking of cat attacks: *Eeeek!*

    a. You carry catnip with you at all times.

    b. You carry a push-pin with you at all times.

    c. You carry a tune with you at all times.

7. Which is your favourite book, now that you are teeny tiny?

    a. *Alice's Adventures in Wonderland.*

    b. *The Borrowers.*

    c. *Stuart Little.*

8. You take your daily bath . . .

    a. in a puddle.

    b. in the dog's water dish.

    c. in a teacup your sister has thoughtfully set out for you.

       (Checking, first, that it contains water and not scaldingly hot tea.)

9. A robin mistakes you for an earthworm and pecks at your head! You . . .

    a. scream *"BAH!"* at it and it flies away.

    b. wave your arms at it and it flies away.

    c. kick it in its scrawny birdy shins and it flies away.

10. What's the best part about being teeny tiny?

    a. Nothing. You wish you were normal size again.

    b. Your whole life has become an adventure!

    c. Spooking the dog.

SCORING

1. a3 b3 c1	4. a3 b2 c1	7. a3 b4 c5	9. a3 b5 c2
2. a5 b3 c1	5. a3 b5 c2	8. a1 b3 c5	10. a1 b3 c5
3. a5 b3 c1	6. a2 b5 c3		

HOW YOU RATE . . .

15-20 Bite-sized snack. You evaded death by dog and capture by cat. But you got swooped up by an eagle and fed to her chicks. You were very tasty.

21-39 A little bit dead. You almost made it, but you were too short to reach the emergency stop button on the escalator.

40+ Tiny triumph! You've put the *wheee!* in peewee. Now if you can only figure out how to create a 5 cm-tall working toilet.

Mother Goose Meets Her Match

Don't be fooled by that sweet little bonnet. Ma Goose is really the criminal mastermind behind a ruthless ring of ruffians. Will you survive your visit to her turf? Or will you get goosed?

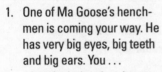

1. One of Ma Goose's henchmen is coming your way. He has very big eyes, big teeth and big ears. You . . .
   a. seek shelter in a house made of straw. Weird — who would use straw to build a house?
   b. seek shelter in a cottage in the woods. Your friend Red's granny lives there.
   c. seek shelter in a cottage in the woods. Awesome — it's made out of candy!
2. Wee Willie Winkie is running all through the town. You . . .
   a. chase after him — he stole your wallet!
   b. wonder where he's going in such a hurry.
   c. call out, "Hey, Wee Willie! Little Boy Blue was looking for you!"
3. Who would you LEAST like to meet up with in Ma Goose's neighbourhood?
   a. Little Bo Peep. There's no telling what that scatterbrain did with her sheep.
   b. Little Miss Muffet. There's no telling what she has hidden in her tuffet. And what's a tuffet anyway?
   c. Little Jack Horner. There's a pretty good reason for him being sent to a corner without the chance of parole for ten years.

4. The cow jumped over the moon. Why?
   a. She was being chased by three blind mice and a farmer's wife with a carving knife.
   b. She didn't want Jack to sell her for some magic beans.
   c. To get to the other side. (Don't tell Chicken Little!)
5. Which magical food item is illegal on Ma Goose's turf?
   a. Pumpkins that turn into coaches.
   b. Beans that turn into super giant beanstalks.
   c. Goose-liver pâté.
6. Who is the worst criminal in Ma Goose's gang?
   a. Goldilocks, because she commits breaking and entering.
   b. Jack Be Nimble, because he commits arson.
   c. The Knave of Hearts, because he steals tarts.
7. What does Ma Goose do to her enemies?
   a. Pushes them off walls. Just ask Humpty Dumpty.
   b. Cuts off their tails. Just ask those three blind mice.
   c. Sends her buddy B. B. Wolf after them. Just ask the three little pigs.
8. Who is Ma Goose's favourite "associate"?
   a. Rumpelstiltskin. Think: Gold!
   b. King Midas. Think: Gold!
   c. Old King Cole. Think: Pipe, drum and fiddlers three!
9. What is Ma Goose's greatest weakness?
   a. Jealousy. Her sister, the Golden Goose, is so much prettier than she is!
   b. Greed. Like that king, she's always in her counting house, counting all her money.
   c. Gluttony. She feasts on blackbirds in pies. And hot cross buns. And muffins from the muffin man.

10. Can you run faster than the Gingerbread Man?
    a. Absolutely. He's a cookie!
    b. Absolutely. Especially since he's waving a giant knife in the air!
    c. Absolutely. Especially since he's been partially eaten by a fox.

SCORING

1. a1 b5 c3	4. a3 b5 c2	7. a3 b4 c2	9. a5 b1 c3
2. a3 b2 c1	5. a1 b1 c5	8. a3 b5 c1	10. a2 b1 c3
3. a5 b1 c3	6. a3 b4 c2		

HOW YOU RATE ...

13-18 You got goosed! We told you not to be fooled by her sweet little bonnet. Mother Goose has taken you down!

19-30 You got game! She's tough, but you're tough too. You've established a truce with the Goose — for now.

31-44 You got gooseland! You did it! You defeated the foul fiend — or fiendish fowl, your choice — on her own territory and have made it your own. All the sheep in the meadow, all the hickory dickory dock clocks, all the ugly ducklings and snoozing princesses and crabby country folk living in shoes — they are all now your responsibility. Go wild, Kid Gosling. (Psst . . . Don't eat the apple, okay?)

Will You Survive Summer Camp?

Ah, the great outdoors. Fresh air, fun friends and — the world's most vicious mosquitoes. Will you survive your summer at Camp Cooties?

1. You think having to use an outhouse is . . .
   a. revolting.
   b. no biggie.
   c. what's an outhouse?
2. Your cabin mate has it in for you! You . . .
   a. complain to the counsellor.
   b. short-sheet his bed when no one is looking.
   c. challenge him to an arm-wrestling contest — in front of the whole camp!
3. Your cabin is going on an overnight trip — canoeing to Ghost Lake! You . . .
   a. can't wait. You've got loads of ghost stories to tell at Ghost Lake.
   b. dread it. You hate canoeing!
   c. can't wait. Nothing better than a long day of paddling followed by yummy s'mores over the campfire.
4. Which activity appeals to you most?
   a. Reading in bed.
   b. Archery.
   c. Swimming.
5. What is "bug juice"?
   a. Fruit juice.
   b. The glop left on your arm after you've slapped at a mosquito.
   c. Insect repellant.
6. You love . . .
   a. your privacy.
   b. diving into icy cold water first thing in the morning.
   c. making funky crafts with string and bark.

7. What is a J-stroke?
   a. A handwriting technique.
   b. A paddling technique.
   c. A tennis technique.
8. Which bunk would you choose?
   a. The top bunk — so no one pees on you.
   b. The bottom bunk — because you're afraid of heights.
   c. The bunk nearest the door — so you can get to the outhouse
      first every morning.

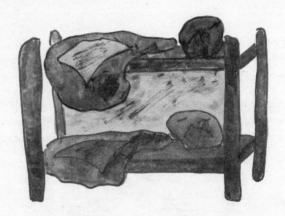

9. Your cabin has decided to go on a midnight raid to scare the kids in the
   Trailblazers cabin. You . . .
   a. plan and lead the raid
   b. sigh. You probably won't get much sleep tonight.
   c. are so excited! You've never been on a raid before and it sounds
      like lots of fun!
10. You're assigned to cabin cleanup! Your cabin wins . . .
    a. neatest.
    b. fastest cleanup crew.
    c. most creatively "decorated." That door-wreath you made out of
       friendless socks? Priceless.